My name is Anna. I work on the checkout at
Morrisons.

When I start work in the morning the first thing I do is to go through the staff only doors. Upstairs there are cloakrooms and loos. I hang up my coat and then I have to clock in.

Everyone who works here has their own card. At the beginning of your shift you find your card on the board and put it in the machine. The machine stamps your card and records what time you started work.

At the end of your shift you have to clock out. That way, there is a record of who is in the building and it means that you'll be paid the correct amount at the end of the month. If you forget to clock in you won't get paid!

Checkout Assistant

Acknowledgements: without the support of the amazing team of staff and management at Morrisons Shrewsbury this book would not have been possible.

First published in Great Britain by Axis Education Ltd.

Printed and bound in the UK by PublishPoint from KnowledgePoint Limited, Reading.

ISBN 978-1-84618-288-4

Axis Education, PO Box 459
Shrewsbury, SY4 4WZ

Email: enquiries@axiseducation.co.uk

www.axiseducation.co.uk

Once I've clocked in I go down to the shop floor and report to my supervisor. He or she will tell me which till I'm going to be working on. Then I go to the till and get ready for work.

I switch the till on and sign in using my password. I check that I've got enough bags. I also make sure I've got enough change and that the belt is running properly. Then I'm ready for customers.

When a customer comes to my till the first thing I do is say hello and ask if they need any help packing their bags.

I move the belt so that the customer has enough space to load their shopping. When the customer is ready, I start scanning the goods.

Once you've been using the machine for a while you get really quick at scanning. It's important to scan the goods quickly because customers don't like to be kept waiting.

You have to take care when you use the scanner. You don't want to scan things twice, or the customer will be charged too much. I can't sort that kind of thing out at the till.

If the supervisor can't fix it, the customer will have to go to the customer services desk to have the receipt checked and to get a refund. That would cause them hassle and extra time and it doesn't give a very good impression either. So while you need to be quick at scanning, you shouldn't rush it either.

I have some regular customers that choose to put their shopping through my till every time they come to the store. They like to have a chat and you get to know them after a while.

Not all goods can be scanned. In-store baked bread rolls don't come with a barcode. You have to know the names of each type of bread roll so that you can tell the till.

The till can weigh goods too. When a customer buys loose fruit or vegetables you put the bag on the scales and tell the till what the product is. That way, the computer can work out the price.

Our store has a fantastic choice of fruit and veg. It's great for the customers as there is so much to buy. We seem to sell vegetables of every different colour, including purple!

This massive choice means that we have to learn what all the weird and wonderful vegetables are. I happen to know that this one is a dudhi. Don't ask me how to cook it though!

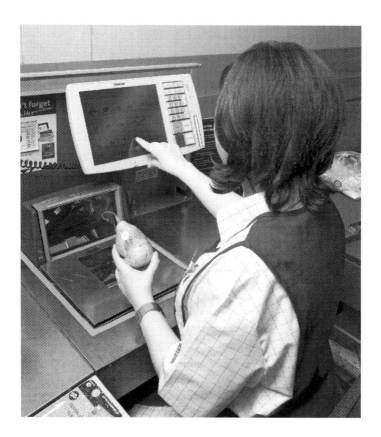

Sometimes a product just won't scan. This is usually because the label is twisted, or the product is an odd shape. When that happens you have to put the barcode in by hand. You need to do this really carefully to make sure the customer is charged for the right product.

If a product doesn't have a barcode and it's not something that's a loose weight item, then I have to call a supervisor. I have a button that makes the light above my till flash.

The supervisors work behind the row of tills so they can see if a light is flashing. They come over and find out what the problem is. Usually they just have to go back to the aisle where the product came from to find the barcode number. I carry on scanning until they come back.

Some goods have a security tag. We have a
machine to remove the tags. They are
magnetic and the machine releases the
magnet so you can remove the tag. If you

don't take the tag off an alarm will sound when the item leaves the store.

Sometimes customers like you to help them with their packing. I always make sure I do this carefully. I try to keep certain types of goods together. I'll pack all of the fruit and veg together in a bag. I'll keep heavy goods like cans and bottles separate from softer goods that could get crushed – such as bread and cakes.

It's important to keep chilled and frozen goods together too.

I like taking pride in my work. Customers spend their hard earned cash on our products. When I make sure that their shopping is scanned accurately and packed carefully it shows that we value their custom.

To be good at this job you have to be polite and friendly with a ready smile. You don't have to be really outgoing – no-one wants to stop for hours chatting at the checkouts. But

I enjoy meeting people, so if you're naturally friendly and helpful, you'd like this job.

When you work on the till, there are some rules that you have to know. There are age limits for some products. It's against the law to sell knives to anyone under 18 and you can't sell them alcohol either.

If someone wants to buy alcohol and they look under 25 you have to ask them to show you some ID. Most people have no problem with this!

When I finish scanning the goods for a customer the till works out the total. It even works out any discounts when we have offers on like buy one, get one free.

Lots of people these days seem to pay with a card. It took customers a while to get used to the chip and pin machine, but it's much quicker than using the old manual machine or writing a cheque.

During the day we take quite a bit of cash, so you still have to be able to handle money. The till will tell you how much change to give, so you need to be able to put the right notes and coins together when you give out change.

We take a lot of cash during the day which has to be sent up to the cash office. We put the money in a pod and there is a really clever system that sucks the pods away. The pods travel down pipes straight to the cash office – we don't even have to leave the till!

During the day I get a couple of breaks. I usually go up to the canteen and have a cup of tea and a chat with my work mates. One of the best things about working here is being with my co-workers. We always have a good laugh.

If we're lucky we can have a quick chat while we're working too. Though usually we're so busy that we don't get the chance. It's good to have someone on hand if you've got a query though.

Working here is perfect for me. My hours are 9.30 until 5.30, five days a week – it's ideal for my home life. Both the staff and customers are great to work with. The uniform is a real bonus – you don't have to wear out your own clothes at work.

At the end of my shift I sign off the till and shut the security gate. I'll look forward to doing the same again tomorrow!

Glossary

barcode – a small rectangle of black lines that contains information that can be read by a computer, usually the price

chip and pin – a way to pay for goods using a credit card and a secret number

clock in – when you register for work at the start of a shift

clock out – when you register that you are leaving work

dudhi – a small pumpkin with green skin and white flesh

supervisor – someone who is in charge of others to make sure that work is being carried out correctly